GRACE'S GROCERIES:
An Introduction to Intuitive Eating

GRACE'S GROCERIES:
An Introduction to Intuitive Eating

Written by: Lexie Kattelman
Illustrated by: Andrea Jane

Today was grocery day! Grace opened her eyes and jumped out of bed. She loved going grocery shopping.

Grace ran to the kitchen and helped her mom with breakfast. Together they made pancakes, eggs, and bacon. Her mom helped her cut strawberries to go with the pancakes.

She even helped pour the orange juice, which had always been her favorite.

When they finished breakfast, her mom grabbed her purse and they went out the door. Grace jumped in the car and quickly buckled her seatbelt.

As they drove, she started thinking about all the different foods they would get at the store.

They turned the corner and there it was! The big brick store with bright red doors.

Grace was so excited! She could already see the shopping carts lined up and ready. Grace loved to push the cart.

Her mom helped her pick out colorful fruits and vegetables. This time, they got apples, bananas, blueberries, avocados, tomatoes, lettuce, and carrots.

Up next was the cereal. Grace's mom always let her choose a box she wanted to take home. This time she chose cinnamon sugar cereal, which sounded delicious.

She lifted the box off the shelf and added it to the cart. She thought about how crunchy and sweet it would be for breakfast or as a snack.

On the next aisle, Grace learned that there were so many fun noodles! Some were long, some were curled, some were short, and some were curved. There were even colorful noodles!

Her mom grabbed a package of noodles from the top shelf and Grace continued to help push the grocery cart through the store.

They added lots of foods to the cart like
sausage, milk, pizza, salad, chips, and yogurt.

Before they got to the check out, they had one last item to choose: a treat from the bakery.

There were cakes, muffins, donuts, pies, and cookies. Grace and her mom decided to each choose a colorful sprinkled donut before they left.

Soon, the shopping cart was so full Grace could barely push it without her mom's help. Their family needed so much food!

While at the checkstand, Grace noticed the
cashier looked different than her. Grace was short
and small and the cashier was tall and large.
Grace saw how happy and helpful the cashier was
as she and her mom bagged the groceries.

Grace pushed the cart full of grocery bags to the car with the help of her mom and asked why some people's bodies looked different.

On the drive home, her mom explained that some people's bodies are tall, some are short, some are curvy, and some are smaller - kind of like all the noodles they saw in the store.

Grace's mom said that all different bodies are good and that they come in all shapes and sizes.

Because we have a body, we can run, jump, dance and play! Bodies are more than something to look at.

Back at home, Grace's mom opened the fridge
to put in the groceries. Grace saw how many
different foods they had. She knew that none
of the food was good or bad and that different
foods help her body in different ways.

Grace's mom thanked her for her help at the grocery store and told her it was time for lunch. Grace's stomach was starting to growl and she knew she was hungry.

After all, the trip to the grocery store was so they could continue taking care of their bodies.

ABOUT THE AUTHOR AND ILLUSTRATOR:

Lexie and Andrea both grew up in Kaysville, Utah. The story is centered around Grace, Andrea's younger sister and Lexie's childhood best friend. After recovering from their own eating disorders, both Lexie and Andrea were introduced to Intuitive Eating.

Lexie has a B.S. in Psychology and a M.S. in Clinical Mental Health Counseling. She currently works as a therapist helping others heal their relationships with food and their body. Through 'Grace's Groceries,' Lexie hopes that caregivers can start early conversations with children about body neutrality and Intuitive Eating including listening to their hunger, discovering satisfaction, feeling their fullness, respecting their bodies, and honoring their health with gentle nutrition.

Andrea has a B.A. in Art with an emphasis in Illustration. She currently works as a floral designer and enjoys making beautiful things everyday. This was a passion project for her as she believes in the ideals of this story and the idea of early introduction of Intuitive Eating into children's lives. Andrea hopes that this book will assist in that process.

Made in the USA
Coppell, TX
06 December 2024